TEETH

Contents

What are teeth for?

Can you think of the different ways in which you use your teeth?

You use your teeth to bite and chew your food before you swallow it. If you had no teeth, you'd only be able to eat soft, mushy foods.

You also use your teeth when you talk. Say the sound "t." Can you feel your tongue pressing against the back of your top teeth? If you had no teeth, you wouldn't be able to say the sound "t." Try saying lots of different words. Imagine what they would sound like if you didn't have teeth.

▷ What do you think you would look like without any teeth?

It is important to care for your teeth because you need them for eating and talking. You also need teeth that look good, because they are an important part of your face. Clean, healthy teeth make you feel and look nice, especially when you smile.

△ Watch other people when they talk, laugh and sing. You can see their teeth.

5

Teeth and gums

The hard bone inside your head is your **skull**. Your teeth are firmly fixed into a part of your skull called the **jawbones**. Half your teeth are in the top jaw. The other half are in the bottom jaw.

The jawbones are covered by your **gums**. This is the pink skin all around your teeth. Your teeth grow through your gums.

▷ This picture shows the skull from the side. You can see the teeth fixed into the jaw-bones.

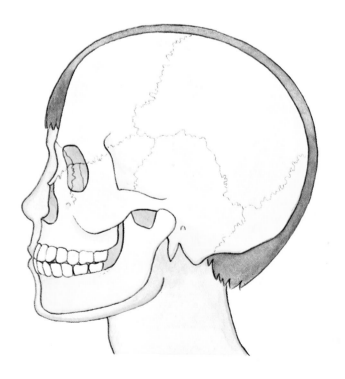

You grow just two sets of teeth. The first set is called the "milk teeth." There are 20 teeth in this set. They start to fall out when you are about six. Do you remember when your milk teeth started to fall out? You could feel new teeth coming through in the gaps. These are the second set of teeth. You will have 32 teeth in this second set.

▽ This baby has only got two teeth. When babies grow their teeth it is called "teething." The six-year-old boy has lost some of his milk teeth. The fourteen-year-old girl has lost all of her milk teeth. Most of her second teeth have come through, but she won't have all of them until she is much older.

The parts of a tooth

When you look at a tooth, you can only see the top half of it. The rest of the tooth is hidden under the gum.

The part you can see is called the **crown**. The part under the gum is called the **root**. The root is the part of the tooth which is fixed into the jawbone. All of your teeth have roots. Each front tooth has just one root. Some back teeth have two roots and some have three roots.

▽ Look at your teeth in a mirror. The only part you can see is the crown of each tooth. The roots are hidden under the gums.

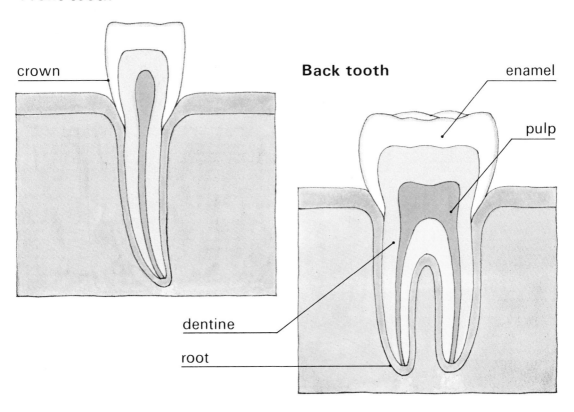

Front tooth

crown

Back tooth

enamel

pulp

dentine

root

A tooth is not the same all the way through. The white outside which you can see is very hard. Under that is a layer like bone. Right in the middle the tooth is very soft. There are **nerves** and **blood vessels** inside the soft part.

△ These pictures show a front and a back tooth cut in half. The white **enamel** on the outside is very hard. The **dentine** is like bone. The **pulp** is very soft.

Teeth for cutting and ripping

Some food that you eat is too big to fit into your mouth in one piece. You need to cut and rip pieces of the food so that it will fit into your mouth.

You have two kinds of teeth which cut and rip food. The teeth that do the cutting are called the **incisors**. There are eight incisors. Four are at the top and four are at the bottom.

▽ Your front teeth are your cutting and ripping teeth. You move your bottom jaw up and down when you bite.

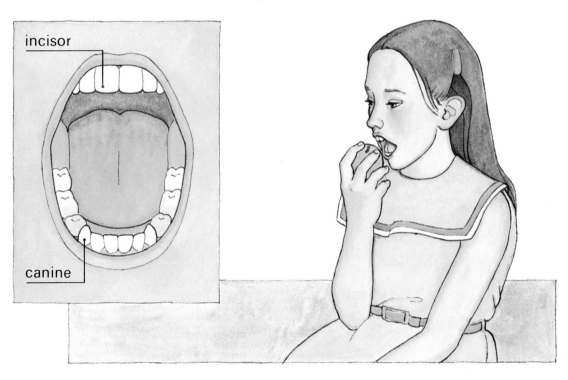

incisor

canine

The teeth that do the ripping are called the **canines**. You have four canines. Two are at the top and two are at the bottom.

If you didn't have these teeth, you would have to cut or break some foods before eating them. Babies who haven't grown their front teeth need all their food chopped into small pieces.

▽ Your cutting and ripping teeth do the same job as a knife. They chop big pieces of food into smaller pieces.

Teeth for grinding

Some of your teeth grind your food when you chew it. The teeth that do the grinding are called **molars**. You can see they are wider than your front teeth. You have eight molars in your first set.

When you are about six, you grow four more molars. These belong to your second set of teeth. They are called "six-year molars."

▽ Your bottom jaw moves up and down and from side to side when you chew. As you chew, your molars grind your food.

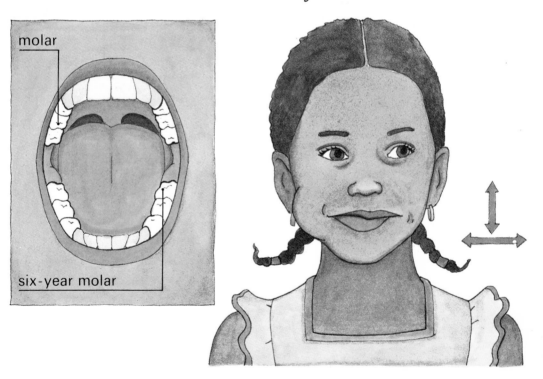

molar

six-year molar

12

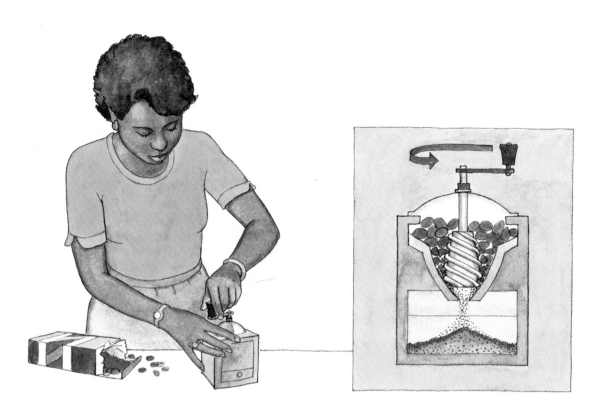

Your grinding teeth are wide on top. They grind food by rubbing it between top and bottom teeth. When you are chewing, your jaw moves up and down and from side to side.

If you didn't have any grinding teeth, you would only be able to eat very soft food.

△ Your grinding teeth do the same job as some appliances in the kitchen. People use grinders to break food into very small pieces.

What is plaque?

Have you ever noticed how crumbs get stuck to your teeth when you eat cookies? Sometimes when you eat an apple, bits get stuck between your teeth. Bits of food often get caught around your teeth when you eat. They are easy to see and feel, and easy to clean away.

▷ This boy is about to chew a disclosing tablet. This has dye in it which makes plaque turn red. You can get disclosing tablets from your dentist or a drugstore.

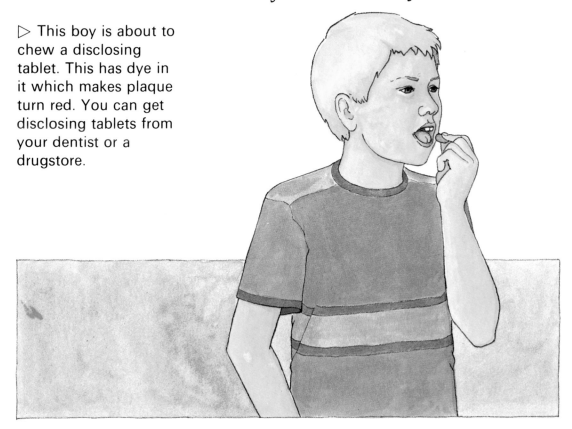

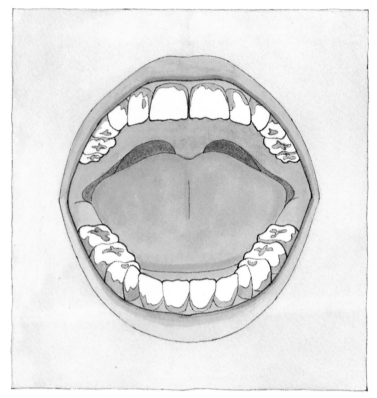

◁ This is what happens when you chew a disclosing tablet. The red dye shows where plaque is on your teeth. You must brush carefully to get rid of the red-stained plaque.

As well as bits of food, there are germs in your mouth. These germs are called bacteria. They are far too small for you to see. They form a sticky layer on your teeth. This layer is called **plaque**.

Plaque will harm your teeth and gums if it is not cleaned off.

Looking after your gums

It is important to look after your gums as well as your teeth. If you don't keep your gums healthy, then your teeth may become wobbly and loose.

The bacteria in plaque can harm your gums. If you don't brush the plaque off your teeth, your gums may get sore and red. This soreness can spread down the sides of the tooth and gum.

▷ Good strong teeth need healthy gums. If gums are not healthy, then good teeth may be lost. It is up to you to make sure you have good gums and teeth.

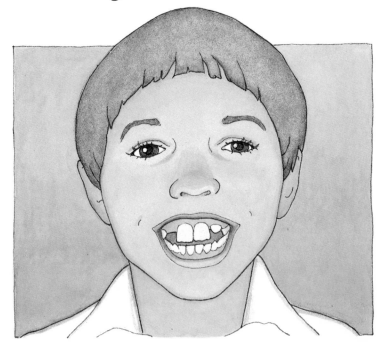

Then a gap can form between the tooth and gum. Bacteria can get into the space. It will be hard to get the plaque out of the space. The tooth will become loose and may have to be taken out.

You can look after your gums by cleaning off all the plaque.

▽ This is how plaque harms gums.
1 You can see plaque around the tooth. It makes the gum sore and red.
2 A space forms between the tooth and gum. Plaque builds up in the gap. The tooth becomes loose.

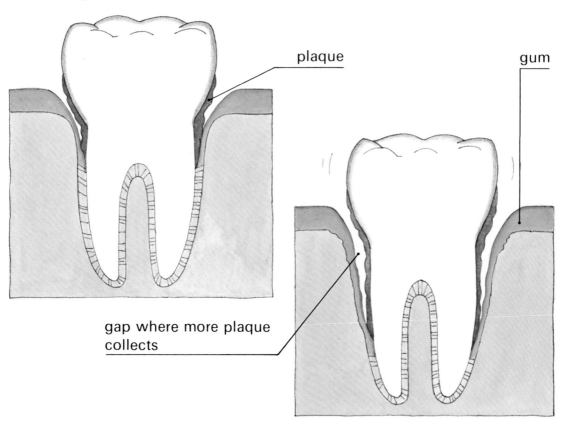

plaque

gum

gap where more plaque collects

Cleaning your teeth

It is important to brush all the plaque off your teeth. You need a good toothbrush and toothpaste.

Your toothbrush should have rounded **tufts** which are not too hard. When the tufts lose their shape, it's time for a new toothbrush.

Most toothpastes have **fluoride** in them. This helps to keep teeth strong.

Make sure you brush your teeth well every day. Brush them after breakfast and at bedtime. Ask a grown-up to help you make sure you are cleaning all your teeth properly.

▽ Use a toothbrush and toothpaste to clean your teeth. **Dental floss** is used to clean between teeth.

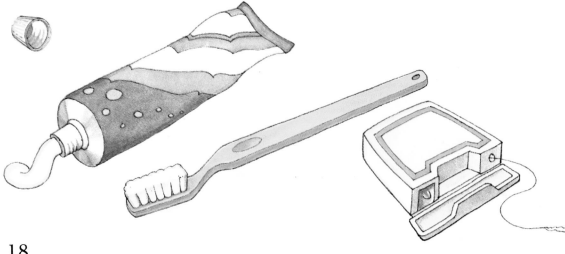

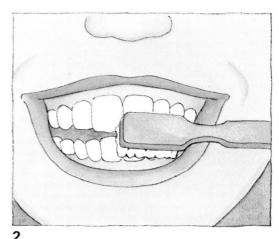

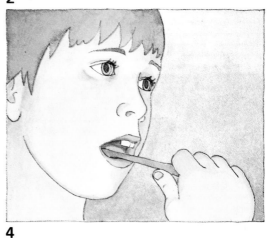

△ How to brush your teeth.
1 Start with the brush tufts where your teeth and gums meet.
2 Move your brush gently in circles. Brush the outside of all your top and bottom teeth.
3 Brush the inside of all your teeth. Make sure you brush the backs of all your front teeth.
4 Brush along the tops of all your back teeth.

19

Sugary foods

Do you like sweet things? Most people do! Unfortunately the sugar which makes them taste sweet is not good for your teeth. The worst thing that you can do is to eat sugary things all day. If you like sweet foods, the best time to eat them is at mealtimes . . . and then clean your teeth.

▽ Candy, chocolate, cookies and cakes all have sugar in them. Most carbonated drinks also have a lot of sugar.

The sugar in foods harms teeth when it mixes with plaque. Sugar and plaque together make **acid**. The acid begins to make very small holes in the teeth.

These holes will get bigger as more sugar and plaque make acid. This is called tooth **decay**. Teeth with decay may begin to hurt.

▽ How sugar attacks a tooth.
1 Acid is made when sugar mixes with plaque.
2 The acid starts to make small holes in the enamel.
3 The holes get bigger as more acid is made. The tooth starts to decay.

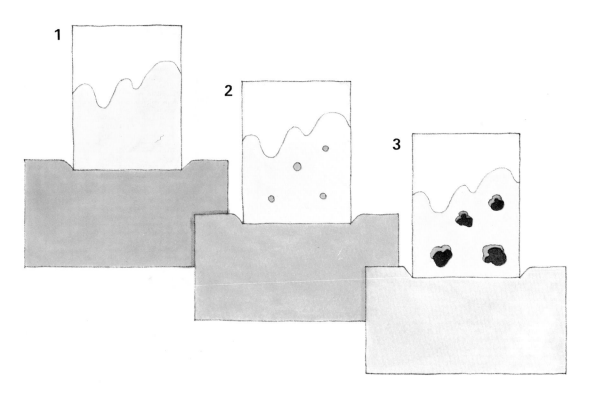

Safe snacks

Sometimes you feel hungry between meals and want something to eat. If you're hungry, it's much better to have a snack that doesn't contain sugar.

There are lots of things you can eat that are safe for your teeth. Some people like eating carrots and celery.

▽ Fresh fruit, celery, carrots, potato chips and nuts are all safe snacks for your teeth.

Other people like fruit and nuts. Cheese is another food which is safe for your teeth.

Next time you want a snack try one of these foods. They will stop you feeling hungry. You will also know that you are looking after your teeth.

△ When you meet your friends at recess or lunchtime, you can share your healthy snacks with them.

Going to your dentist

You can do a lot to look after your teeth. If you brush them very carefully and do not eat too many sugary foods, you will be helping yourself.

Your dentist can also help you to look after your teeth. He or she will be able to check that they are all strong and healthy. If there is anything wrong, the dentist will be able to fix your teeth before the harm goes too far.

▷ When you visit your dentist, you will be shown to the waiting room and the dentist will be told that you are there. The dentist has assistants who keep records about your teeth. They also help the dentist when she examines your teeth.

You should visit your dentist at least twice a year. Don't wait until you have a toothache or sore gums. Go for all your check-ups and your dentist will be able to help you to look after your teeth.

▽ This girl is having her teeth scaled and polished to make sure they are really clean. The dentist can tip the chair back so that she can see into the mouth.

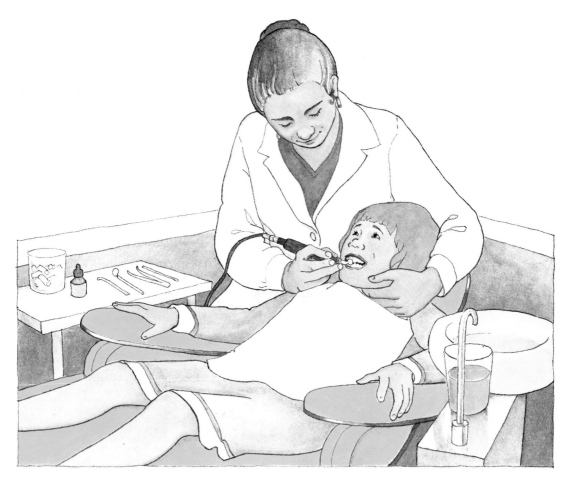

What your dentist can do

There are many ways your dentist can help you. He can show you how to clean your teeth properly. If he finds some tooth decay, he can drill it out and fill the hole.

If your teeth are crooked, he can fit **braces** to straighten them. Braces are thin bands of metal. Sometimes teeth may be too crowded. Then he can take some out to make room for others to grow properly.

Your teeth may get broken by accident. Then your dentist can fit a new crown to the broken tooth.

△ How a tooth is filled.
1 This is the decay.
2 The tooth is drilled to get rid of all the decay. The dentist gives an injection in the gum so that the drilling doesn't hurt.
3 The dentist puts a filling in the tooth.

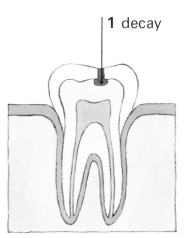

1 decay

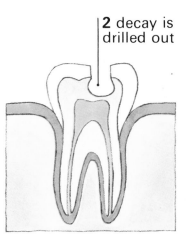

2 decay is drilled out

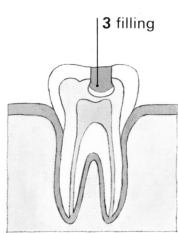

3 filling

wax

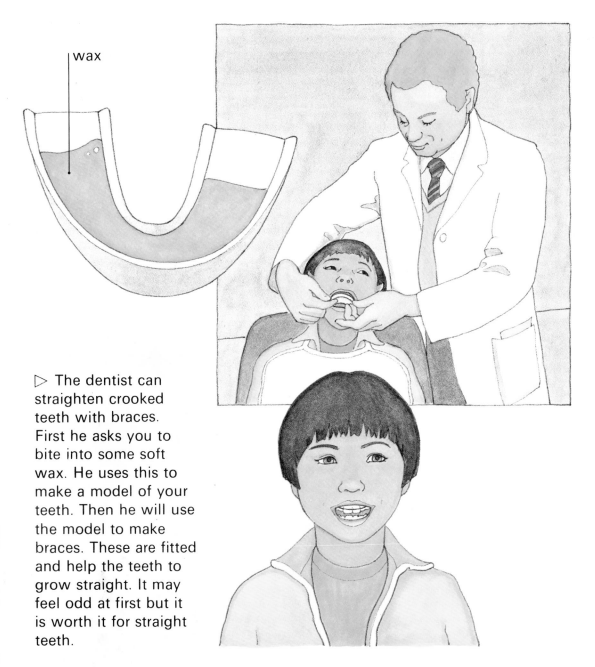

▷ The dentist can straighten crooked teeth with braces. First he asks you to bite into some soft wax. He uses this to make a model of your teeth. Then he will use the model to make braces. These are fitted and help the teeth to grow straight. It may feel odd at first but it is worth it for straight teeth.

Things to do

1 Find out how well you are cleaning your teeth. Get some disclosing tablets from a drugstore. Chew one of the tablets. The dye in it will stain the plaque red. Use a mirror to see where the plaque is sticking to your teeth. Then use your toothbrush and toothpaste to clean your teeth. Check how well you are cleaning your teeth by using a disclosing tablet once a week. Do this for 3 or 4 weeks. Then check every month to make sure you are really brushing well and getting rid of all the plaque.

2 Make a chart showing the parts of your teeth where it is hard to get rid of plaque. This will remind you of the places where you have to take special care to clean well. You can also write down the dates when you need to check your cleaning with a disclosing tablet.

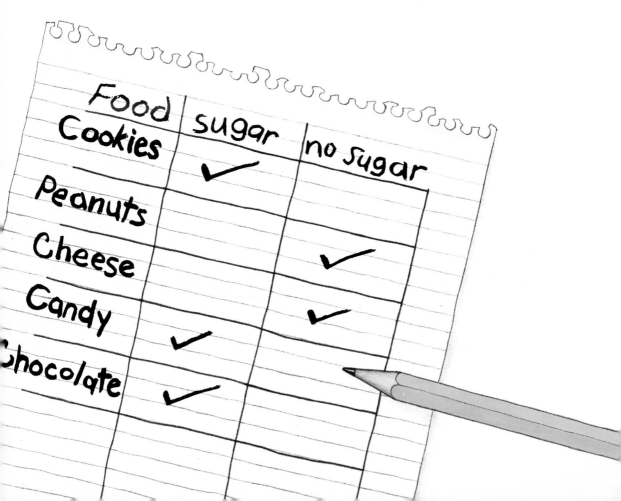

Food	sugar	no sugar
Cookies	✓	
Peanuts		
Cheese		✓
Candy		✓
Chocolate	✓	

3 Look at the packets and wrappers of different foods. They will have lists of ingredients. These tell you what is in the food. Make a chart to show which foods have sugar in them and which do not.

4 Make a list of all the snacks you eat between meals. How many of them contain sugar? Do you think you are eating too many sugary foods between meals? Make a plan to start eating some safer snacks.

Glossary

Acid What is made when the bacteria in plaque feed on sugar. It can make holes in teeth.

Blood vessels The tubes which carry blood all over the body. There are blood vessels inside each tooth.

Braces Bands of metal fitted to teeth to help them grow straight.

Canines The big pointed teeth at the front. There are two at the top and two at the bottom.

Crown The upper part of the tooth which you can see.

Decay This is what happens when you get holes in your teeth. Decay starts in the enamel. It spreads to the dentine and pulp if it is not drilled out.

Dental floss Special thread for cleaning between the teeth. You should ask your dentist before using it.

Dentine The middle layer of a tooth. It is strong like bone but not as hard as enamel.

Disclosing tablets

Tablets made with a food dye. They stain plaque red so that you can see it.

Enamel The white layer on the outside of a tooth. It is very, very hard.

Fluoride A chemical which is found in drinking water. It can help strengthen teeth against decay. Most toothpastes contain fluoride.

Gums These cover the jawbones and the roots of the teeth. Teeth grow through the gums.

Incisors The front teeth used for cutting food. There are four at the top and four at the bottom in both the first and second sets of teeth.

Jawbones The parts of the skull which teeth are fixed into. Only the lower jaw-bone can move. It is joined to the skull by a hinge.

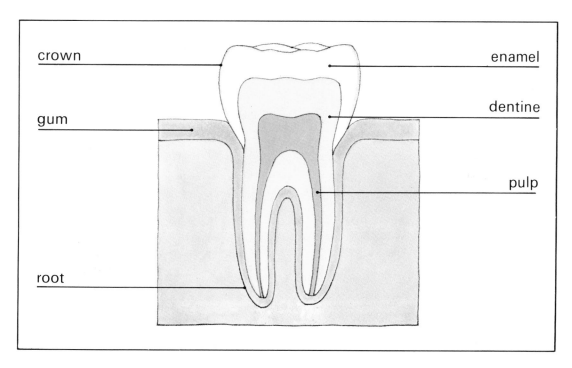

crown — enamel

dentine

gum

pulp

root

Molars These are the back teeth. They are used for grinding food. There are eight in the first set of teeth. Four more molars grow at about the age of six. These are part of the second set of teeth. There are 20 molars in this second set.

Nerves There are nerves all over your body. Some carry messages to your brain. The nerves in your teeth send messages about hot and cold, touch and pain.

Plaque This is a thin sticky layer of bacteria on the teeth. It is very hard to see on its own.

Pulp The very soft middle part of a tooth. There are nerves and blood vessels inside it.

Root The lower half of the tooth. It is under the gum and cannot be seen. The root is the part of the tooth which is fixed into the jaw bone.

Skull This is the name given to all the bones of the head.

Tufts These are the bristles on a tooth-brush.

Index

PRINTED IN BELGIUM BY
proost
INTERNATIONAL BOOK PRODUCTION